Protect
Nature

Kay Barnham

WAYLAND

Copyright © Wayland 2006
Editor: Penny Worms
Senior Design Manager: Rosamund Saunders
Designer: Ben Ruocco, Tall Tree Ltd

Published in Great Britain in 2006 by Wayland,
an imprint of Hachette Children's Books

British Library Cataloguing in Publication Data
Barnham, Kay
    Protecting nature. - (Environment action)
    1. Nature conservation - Juvenile literature
    I. Title
    333.9'516

ISBN 10: 0 7502 4869 6
ISBN 13: 978 0 7502 4869 3

Printed in China
Wayland
An imprint of Hachette Children's Books
338 Euston Road, London NW1 3BH

The publishers would like to thank the following for allowing us to
reproduce their pictures in this book:
Alamy images: 18 (John White Photos). Corbis images: 19 (Galen Rowell),
21 (Grace/zefa). Ecoscene: title page and 12 (Reinhard Dirscherl),
5 (Frank Blackburn), 6 (David Wootton Photography), 7 (Kjell Sandved),
9 (Reinhard Dirscherl), 10 (Luc Hosten), 13 (Andy Binns), 14 (Wayne
Lawler), 15 (Robert Baldwin), 17 (Edward Bent), 22 (Stephen Coyne), 23
(Satyendra Tiwari), 24 (Sally Morgan), 25 (Frank Blackburn), 26 (Angela
Hampton), 29 (Angela Hampton). Getty images: 4 (Johnny Johnson), 8
(Michael S Quinton), 11 (Michael Kelley), 16 (Daryl Balfour), 27 (Arthur
Tilley). Photolibrary: cover and 28 (Satushek Steve).
Wayland Picture Library: 20.

Contents

All About Nature

Nature is the word used to describe the world around us. Natural things are not made by people – they are plants, animals, the **landscape** and the sea.

△ The best place to see nature at its most beautiful is far away from people, like in this Canadian wilderness.

You can see nature in towns and cities too. Trees, flowers and insects are all part of the natural world. Next time you are outside, take a look around. How many natural things can you see?

△ Even the smallest flowers and insects are part of nature.

Is Nature in Danger?

Millions of people live on our planet. They need space to live and food to eat. They use **fuel** to heat their homes and run their cars. They make paper from trees and use land for farming. They throw away rubbish. All of these **human activities** put nature in danger.

△ When new houses are built, parts of the countryside are destroyed.

> Giant pandas are in danger of becoming extinct. Huge areas of the bamboo forests in which they live have been lost or cut down.

Natural habitats are places where animals and plants live. When their natural habitat is changed or destroyed, the animals and plants have to move or adapt. Some may become **extinct**. This means that they are gone for ever.

Climate Change

Our planet is getting warmer. Many experts believe that this climate change is caused by **carbon dioxide** from power stations, factories, houses, aeroplanes and cars. This gas is sent into the earth's **atmosphere**, trapping the sun's heat. Deserts could grow bigger. Sea levels could rise, flooding low-lying islands.

American pikas are small animals that live on cool mountaintops. If the temperature rises too much, they may become extinct.

FACT!

Some scientists believe that this **global warming** could threaten over a million animal and plant **species**.

Higher sea temperatures harm **fragile coral** that lives in tropical seas. If the water becomes warmer, the colourful coral fades and dies. Warm seas also lead to more powerful **hurricanes** and storms – the rough seas can cause serious damage to coral.

△ Coral reefs are home to lots of different sea creatures.

A Cleaner World

Pollution can cause great harm to wildlife and natural habitats. For example, when factories pour **poisonous waste** into seas, rivers and lakes, fish and other creatures may become ill or die. Many people would like to make sure that this pollution is stopped.

△ Plastic rubbish dumped into the ocean can kill birds and sea creatures, by choking, poisoning or strangling them.

Rubbish can take hundreds of years to rot and disappear. Some rubbish never rots. By **reducing**, **re-using** and **recycling** waste, we can help to make our planet a cleaner place.

△ Food and drinks packaging causes most of the litter you see in the countryside and around towns. Take it home and recycle it!

Natural Habitats

People have already destroyed natural habitats to make way for houses and farmland. Large areas of **rainforest** have been chopped down to make furniture and paper.

△ As rainforests become smaller, orang-utans are in great danger of becoming extinct.

◁ This tree nursery in Nepal is planting thousands of trees to replace those cut down.

FACT!

In the UK, there are more than twice as many trees as a hundred years ago.

The **destruction** of forests can cause other problems, such as flooding and mudslides. Bare hillsides allow rain to run down them much faster, which can raise river levels quickly or wash away soil.

Endangered Animals

Giant pandas, tigers, whales, dolphins, rhinos, elephants, turtles and gorillas are just some of the world's animals that are in danger of extinction. Some have been killed for their meat, fur and tusks, while some have been hunted for sport. Others have lost their homes.

◁ Fewer than five hundred Sumatran tigers now live in the wild. This is mostly because of hunting.

Today, **endangered** animals are protected. Most live in **nature reserves**, which are areas where they are looked after. This and other important steps are being taken to help provide a better future for these creatures.

 In Ecuador, a new type of fishing hook is used to catch fish. Now, far fewer endangered sea turtles are caught by accident like this one.

Nature Reserves

In nature reserves, wildlife comes first. They have
been created to protect the homes of **rare**
animals and plants. Park rangers take care of the
animals and stop people from harming them.

△ Elephants, impala and
gemsbok roam freely in
Etosha nature reserve in
Namibia, Africa.

Nature reserves are open to the public so that everyone can enjoy the **environment** and see wildlife in its natural habitat. Visitors are welcome, as long as they leave the nature reserve exactly as they found it.

▽ These tourists are visiting Skomer Island nature reserve in Wales. It is home to many sea birds and seals.

Marine Reserves

Some protected areas are not just on land – they include seas, lakes and bays too. These **marine reserves** are places where sea creatures can live in safety. Shipping and fishing are controlled. Drilling for oil and gas, and dumping rubbish are not allowed.

◁ Over-fishing, pollution and loss of habitat mean that some types of fish are now much less common. This includes these Bluefin tuna.

There are lots of marine reserves around the world, but nature lovers would like to see many more. They are ideal places for people to see nature, without spoiling it.

△ Monterey Bay in California, USA, is a protected area of sea and coastline. It is home to sea birds, fish, mammals and plants. This sea otter lives there safely.

Stop, Think, Act!

There are lots of things we can do to protect nature, both around the world and closer to home. Before you buy things, make sure that any natural habitats or wildlife haven't been harmed to make them. For example, if you buy recycled paper, you can be sure that no new trees have been chopped down to make it.

◁ Before you throw things away, stop! Could you recycle them? Cans, cardboard, batteries and plastic are just some of the things that can be recycled.

Many household cleaners contain poisonous **chemicals**. These chemicals harm the environment when they get into our seas and lakes. When you go shopping, look out for **environmentally friendly** or 'green' products. They contain chemicals that dissolve or disappear harmlessly in water.

Protecting Nature on Holiday

Around the world, people have worked hard to make sure that nature is protected. You can help too. When you are on holiday, never buy **souvenirs** that have come from endangered animals or habitats. Ivory ornaments are made from elephant tusks. Hardwood furniture may come from endangered rainforests.

When coral and sponge are taken from the seabed to make souvenirs like these, they die.

When tourists visit wild animals in nature reserves, they are helping to protect nature by giving money to these valuable places. They also provide work for local guides.

Sometimes, wild animals are captured. They may be sold as pets or made to work. This can cause them a lot of distress. It is also very difficult for these animals to learn to live in the wild again. To stop this happening, it is important not to support this illegal activity.

Protecting Nature at Home

There are lots of ways that you can protect nature at home. If you have a garden you could make **compost** instead of throwing scrap food away. Fill a composter with scrap food. When the food has rotted down, it can be spread on soil to feed growing plants.

◁ Things like teabags, fruit peel, eggshells and vegetable peelings can be composted, along with grass cuttings and leaves.

During the cold winter months, why not hang a bird feeder outside to help wild birds survive when they cannot find much food? If you have a cat, make sure it wears a bell, to warn feathery visitors!

▽ Use lots of different types of seed to encourage all sorts of birds.

Protecting Nature at School

When you're at school, there are lots of things you can do to learn about nature and how to protect it. Some schools have vegetable patches, where pupils grow things. Others have birdwatching clubs, where pupils look out for wild birds and learn about them.

◁ You can plant a tree and watch it grow. Note how it changes from season to season and what wildlife it attracts.

An important way that you can protect nature is by making sure that all litter is put into bins – or recycled. As well as making places look ugly and untidy, litter can harm wildlife.

△ Picking up litter is one of the easiest ways you can help protect nature around you.

FACT!

Small animals can get trapped inside bottles or cans. Broken bottles can cut their feet.

More Ideas!

If you have a garden or window box, why not create your own nature garden? There are lots of things you can add to it to encourage wildlife to live and grow there. Ask a gardener which plants will grow well.

△ Flowers will attract bees, butterflies and insects. Small trees and bushes will provide shelter for small creatures like hedgehogs and frogs.

Use a **water butt** or a bucket to collect rainwater. You can use this to water your garden when it is dry.

△ Don't use sprays to control weeds – instead, just let them grow! Some interesting plants may begin to sprout in your nature garden.

FACT!

Don't use peat to grow plants in pots. Peat is taken from precious wild habitats. Instead, use peat-free compost or your own home-made compost.

Glossary

Atmosphere – the air around the earth

Carbon dioxide – a type of gas in the air

Chemicals – powerful liquids or powders that can be used for lots of things, including cleaning

Compost – rotted vegetables and other waste that is added to soil as food for plants

Coral – a kind of rock made in the sea from the bodies of tiny sea creatures

Destruction – when something is totally ruined

Endangered – when the remaining number of a type of animal or plant is very low

Environment – the world we live in, especially plants, animals and nature

Environmentally friendly – products that do not harm the environment

Extinct – when a type of animal or plant dies out so that not one remains alive anywhere in the world

Fragile – easily broken

Fuel – anything that is burnt to make heat

Global warming – when the world becomes a hotter place

Human activities – the things people do

Hurricanes – storms with very strong winds

Landscape – a large area of countryside

Marine reserves – safe areas where sea creatures can live

Natural habitats – places where animals or plants usually live

Nature reserves – safe areas where animals can live without being harmed by human activity

Peat – a type of rich, boggy soil

Poisonous waste – leftover chemicals that can cause death or harm

Pollution – dirty or unhealthy air or water

Rainforest – a large forest in a hot part of the world

Rare – hard to find

Recycling – not throwing something away after use but using it again somehow

Reducing – making something smaller or less

Re-using – using something again

Souvenirs – things that you buy to remind you of a holiday or place

Species – a type of living thing

Water butt – a large barrel that catches rainwater

Index